MILLENNIALS' QUICK GUIDE TO
BEING A BOSS

What No One Ever Told You
About Being a True Leader

WINDING PATHWAY BOOKS

Jennifer P. Wisdom

© 2021 Jennifer P. Wisdom

All rights reserved. No part of this publication may be reproduced, stored in a retrieval system, or transmitted in any form or by any means, electronic, mechanical, photocopying, recording, scanning, or otherwise, except as permitted under Section 107 or 108 of the 1976 International Copyright Act without prior written permission except in brief quotations embodied in critical articles and reviews.

Published by Winding Pathway Books

WINDING PATHWAY BOOKS

ISBN (print): 978-1-954374-27-0
ISBN (e-book): 978-1-954374-26-3

Book design by Wendy C. Garfinkle
Cover design by Diego G. Diaz
Photo Credit: Diego G. Diaz

For more information or bulk orders, visit:
www.millennialsguides.com

Printed in the United States of America

Table of Contents

HOW TO USE THIS QUICK GUIDE — 1

Chapter 1: Be the Boss You Always Wanted — 3

Chapter 2: Hiring Strong Staff — 7

Chapter 3: Developing and Retaining Strong Staff — 13

Chapter 4: Delegating — 19

Chapter 5: Supervising Someone Older Than You — 23

Chapter 6: Communicating Like a Boss — 27

Chapter 7: Acing Difficult Conversations — 31

Chapter 8: Asserting Your Authority — 35

Chapter 9: Conducting Performance Reviews — 39

Chapter 10: Being an Ally, Advocate, and Mentor — 43

Chapter 11: Motivating Staff — 49

Chapter 12: Building the Multicultural Workplace — 53

Chapter 13: Building Belonging — 57

Chapter 14. Using Your Power for Good — 61

ACKNOWLEDGEMENTS — 65

ABOUT THE AUTHOR — 67

HOW TO USE THIS QUICK GUIDE

If you've read other books in the *Millennials' Guides* series (*Millennials' Guide to Work; Millennials' Guide to Management and Leadership; Millennials' & Generation Z Guide to Voting; Millennials' Guide to Relationships; Millennials' Guide to Diversity, Equity & Inclusion;* or *Millennials' Guide to the Construction Trades*), you know how this works. *Millennials' Guides* are not books necessarily best read cover to cover. I encourage you to review the table of contents and identify a challenge you are currently having or recently experienced. Turn to those pages to start finding a solution!

Each chapter in this Quick Guide includes a brief description, several things to think about, and activities that you may want to try. Many times, you can feel improvement after trying one option. You'll see some information repeated across different chapters because they're likely to be helpful for many problems. For complex challenges, you may want to attempt several interventions at the same time.

It's important to have patience and give the solutions and considerations a little bit of time to work. Some ideas that you try won't solve the problem but will make it a little better or make you think differently about the issue --

that's still success! If you don't feel comfortable trying an activity, try something else. Some of the activities are very low risk, such as changing your expectations of other people. Others can appear more challenging. Start with actions that feel like lower risk to you and work your way up to more challenging actions. As you work through the book, you'll get better at understanding how to be a boss; reading situations; responding respectfully to people you work with; building positive and diverse networks; and applying solutions effectively. Observe, be patient, clarify your own boundaries, and learn. The goal of the strategies in this book is to help you develop skills that will serve you well as you continue to move forward in your lifelong exploration of being a boss.

Each of you reading this Quick Guide is a unique person with talents to share with the world. My hope is that this book can make it easier for you to do so. Good luck improving the world!

Chapter 1: Be the Boss You Always Wanted

When you think of the best boss you ever had, or an exceptional boss from a movie, television show or book, you know what it means to be a great boss. Similarly, when you think of your experiences and the many examples of awful bosses from the media, you know what a terrible boss is too. If you want to be an amazing boss, you need to look at yourself first. What does being a good boss mean? What kind of a boss do you want to be? Right now, you can start being a great boss by setting an example and making changes in your own life that you want to see reflected in your community, society, and in the world. Let's do this!

1. **Self-evaluation** is an important process in order to make positive changes in ourselves. Look at the areas within yourself that you think are great, and the areas in which you'd like to grow. These can include specific skills, like programming or public speaking, and also skills like kindness, patience, generosity, and precision. Self-evaluation can help you become aware of habits you might not have even recognized before that you want to change.
2. **Become aware of self-talk and language you use towards others.** If you want to see more respect in

your workplace, check to see if you are being respectful in your own self-talk and in the language you use with your colleagues. Be patient and kind to yourself as you start to change your life for the better – and as you start to improve your workplace for everyone!

3. **Learn from others.** If you want to make changes in yourself it's helpful to research and learn about how others made changes in their lives and gain insights. Learn from the best bosses, and also learn from others' mistakes and bad habits. Listen to podcasts and read books and articles about people making positive change and doing good in the world.

4. **Create positive habits that reinforce the change you wish to see in yourself and others.** Kindness is a habit that can be added into your daily life: it can start small and evolve from there. You may also want to consider positive habits around eating, sleeping, meditating, reading, exercising, or other activities that can make you stronger.

5. **Step out of your comfort zone.** Many of us have adapted a daily routine that feels safe. Sometimes it's helpful to push to the edge of that comfort zone to grow even as uncomfortable as it may feel. Taking a chance, trying new food, traveling to another country, or daring to be vulnerable push us out of our daily comfort zone. These experiments in being brave can have a positive impact on your

perspectives, what kind of boss you are, and maybe even the way you live your life.

6. **Surround yourself with others who are aligned with the changes you wish to see.** When you are around a group of people who also want to change themselves for the better and make a positive impact it can help foster your own motivation and growth. You can learn from each other and – bonus! – you have a built-in support system.

7. **Use social media for positive change**. Social media such as Twitter, LinkedIn, TikTok, and Instagram can be platforms where you use your voice to share *positive* language, actions, events, knowledge, and experiences. Through social media you can connect with others who are also working towards change for the positive. Setting intentions before using these platforms is helpful to keep your focus on what you're using them for and not getting off-track.

8. **Take action and volunteer.** One of the best activities you can join in is by volunteering for something you truly believe in or wish to learn more about. Volunteering can be for a committee at work, an annual event, or a community organization. Volunteering can also connect you with a community that also wants the changes you wish to see. It not only helps others, but it also helps *you* by changing your mindset and your view of others.

See also:
Chapter 8: Asserting Your Authority
Chapter 13: Building Belonging

Chapter 2: Hiring Strong Staff

The best bosses surround themselves with capable, competent people who soak up feedback, know when to ask questions, and reliably perform at the highest levels. How do you get great staff? Hire great staff!

1. **Many times, people think the most important aspect of hiring is finding someone who can do technical skills, but often that's only a baseline.** Often characteristics such as friendliness, the ability to work well in teams, persistence, humor, and striving for excellence are more important indicators of success. One of my colleagues used to say, "I can teach them how to do the job, but if they are adults who don't listen or can't get along, there's not much I can do to help them!"
2. **It's important to have a good idea of what you are looking for in the position.** Considering technical proficiency as a given, are you looking for someone who can pull together the team, start new areas of inquiry, or plan well? Or are you looking for someone with connections or experience in the industry? Would you consider a candidate with less technical experience but who seems trainable and is a good team player? You may want to discuss with colleagues or your team what kind of person the

position needs and what skills would be most helpful. Know what you want, and go find it!

3. **Consider whether you would like experience vs. raw talent.** Both of these can bring strengths to your team: Individuals with experience are likely to be less reactive and have a broader base of knowledge but may be less willing to take direction. Raw talent may have brains and energy but be more challenging to focus and corral.

4. **Write clear and compelling job descriptions that focus on impact.** Focus your job descriptions on potential impact, what candidates are expected to know, and what candidates could learn on the job instead of a checklist of what characteristics/skills the person should have. You can also identify if required qualifications, such as educational requirements, could be adjusted for people with comparable lived experience. *This is especially important because men typically apply for a job when they meet only 60 percent of the qualifications, whereas women don't feel confident to apply unless they meet 100 percent.*

5. **Hire people who are better than you.** Many leaders and managers worry their protégés might outshine them, so they hire less capable staff who are less threatening. This is a mistake! The best people will rise to the top anyway, and your staff keeping you on your toes isn't the worst thing. Plus, it's wonderful to

be a part of a superstar's meteoric rise (and you get the reflected glory because you were smart enough to hire them). Similarly, find staff who complement your weaker areas, whether they can support you in technical skills, organization, warmth, or other expertise.

6. **Consider who should be included in interviewing a candidate,** and who gets to make the decision. Including all staff in interviewing a candidate can provide the false sense to staff that they all have equal weight in the decision. It also presents to the candidate that decisions are made by a group rather than by the manager. On the other hand, it can present a unified front and a strong ethic of teamwork. Consider what messages you want to send to your staff and to the candidates.

7. **If your boss is pushing a candidate you don't prefer,** you can have the conversation regarding what the team needs and who you think would be best. Be diplomatic and not too harsh about the boss's preferred candidate, because you might get stuck with them anyway. These things aren't always fair.

8. **If you have staff you inherited who are not great, help them become great.** Help those who are not performing at the minimum standard improve skills or move on to find something more appropriate. And work on helping the good staff become great by

motivating them, helping them learn and grow, and praising their success.

9. **Learn how to interview candidates well.** Some organizations have structured interview questions, but most leave managers on their own to improvise. Don't ask easy questions (e.g., "Do you know how to x?"); instead ask about their ability to think and make decisions and collaborate. Ask about challenging situations, a time they struggled with a coworker or boss, and how they would go about approaching a sample realistic task from work. Some managers even give a written prompt for a simulated work task and have the candidate spend 15-30 minutes preparing a written answer. Also probe for their level of self-awareness, including what they need from a boss, and how they need to be successful. The content of their answers is important, but so is their communication style, ease in speaking with you, and awareness of social cues.

10. **Similarly, work with whoever is on the hiring team to reach consensus on how candidates should be evaluated, how resumes should be reviewed, and how interviews should be conducted.** Identify, for example, whether interviewers should focus on accomplishments, growth, conscientiousness, or a combination of these. You may want to help them focus on open-ended questions to help you

understand how candidates approached a situation, not just what was completed.

11. **Hire for diversity -- yes, ethnic/racial and gender diversity -- but also diversity of thought, experience, and approach.** Allow the new hire to retain the uniqueness that you hired them for so they can really contribute to the team's overall success.

12. **Check references, and don't ask only easy questions.** In the U.S., there are some legal limits on what questions you can ask a reference; for example, you can't ask about personal demographic information such as race, religion, pregnancy status, or disability status. You can, however, ask if the employer would hire the candidate again, what the candidate's strengths and weaknesses are, how the candidate got along with colleagues, what it's like to work with the candidate, and what the candidate needs to be most successful. The reference might not provide the information, but you can always ask. Document everything.

13. **Once you find the right person for the job, help them hit the ground running!** Announce their arrival as broadly as appropriate, make sure they have an orientation to your department (in addition to any orientation your organization might provide), and identify who they can go to with questions. Check in with them and with your other staff frequently at

first to see how it's going and to ensure the new person is successful.

See also:
Chapter 3: Developing and Retaining Strong Staff
Chapter 4: Delegating
Chapter 5: Supervising Someone Older Than You

Chapter 3: Developing and Retaining Strong Staff

Most people want to learn and grow. As a boss, you can help your employees with professional development opportunities they might not have considered. Employees understand that being offered professional development opportunities means that you are investing in their careers beyond just what they're doing for you currently; this can improve morale and their loyalty to you.

1. **Tell your staff that you value professional development.** Maximize learning opportunities by requesting or requiring all staff who obtain company-funded training share what they learned with others on the team formally or informally. This doubles as a professional development opportunity in synthesizing information and public speaking!
2. **Model your values of professional development and the importance of lifelong learning.** Share what you learn when you go to training or conferences, send around information from professional associations, and bring up current events in your field during staff meetings so everyone learns all the time.
3. **Ask lots of questions** to help your team start working through a project or tackle a conundrum. Sometimes we get stuck thinking that because we are the

manager or leader that we have to know everything. But it's often better for everyone involved if the boss is asking questions and helping staff figure out things on their own, rather than directing them or micromanaging. By asking questions for your team to work out an answer to, you can understand their thinking processes and provide guidance about inaccurate assumptions or more effective strategies. You might even learn something!

4. **Train staff to bring you solutions, not problems.** If your staff think you're there to solve their problems for them, they will bring you problems. Teach them to bring you potential solutions when they bring you challenges. This will create opportunities for you to provide feedback on their problem-solving strategies.

5. **Provide professional development opportunities in your day-to-day activities.** Here are some examples: delegate a small part of a project or a whole project to a staff member; ask a staff member to report on some component of their work at a small meeting (they can prepare the material and review it with you to get feedback before the meeting); invite a staff member to attend a higher-level meeting to learn more about organizational context (be sure to prepare them for the meeting, ask what they learned, and request they report back to their colleagues in a meeting about their experience).

6. **Find out what training funds or tuition reimbursement may be provided to employees** and whether the organization supports paid time to attend training. Consider professional development in technical areas of your field (e.g., finance, law) and also in soft skills like written communication, leadership, and public speaking. Share this information with your staff and encourage them to take advantage of the opportunities.
7. **Assist staff in identifying their mentoring needs** and provide support around these needs, whether technical or softer skills such as negotiation, communication, or process improvement. For specific technical needs, invite a colleague from another department in your organization to present to your staff and engage them in a discussion about the topic. You can offer to return the favor to their department, possibly including one of your staff as an additional professional development opportunity.
8. **Consider a book club/journal club.** You and your staff might be interested in reading an article or book together or engaging in regular discussion of current events. If so, ask staff members to identify date/time of conversations, distribute the article/book, and facilitate the meeting. You can initially facilitate the meetings to show them how. Use the meetings, however, as an opportunity for others to step up and take responsibility for keeping the meetings going.

9. **Let them make mistakes.** You can't save staff from ever making mistakes, and sometimes you have to let them fail. You can assist them in identifying what went wrong, how to do it differently, and how to manage failure. It's also important to consider the consequences of mistakes – if someone has to stay late and fix the problem, that is a natural and logical consequence. Punishing staff, yelling at them, or making them fearful will NOT keep them from making mistakes; it just makes staff upset and on edge.
10. **Professional associations and federal agencies may have materials or training** available to your staff for them to access individually or as a team training, depending on your field. Introduce your staff to the right content experts, role models, and prospective mentors. Encourage them to build relationships widely and, of course, to pay it forward.
11. **Give stretch assignments,** which are those that are developmentally challenging for a person and require them to work beyond their current skills, but not so far that they feel incompetent and fail. We may be tempted to give every assignment to the person who is best at it, but then others don't get a chance to learn! Consider who is a good fit for the assignment and how you can support them in their learning process (while still being successful with the assignment).

Developing and Retaining Strong Staff

12. **Check in regularly.** Scheduled supervision or 1:1's helps staff feel safe and consistent so that you're not only talking to them when you need to give them critical feedback. Regular meetings (weekly, monthly, or quarterly) allow you to develop a relationship, get updates on tasks, reassess needs, and answer questions.
13. **Help your staff navigate office politics.** The best content knowledge won't help someone with politics, and junior staff often need help recognizing politics and learning how to respond in a savvy manner. You can bring some political challenges (possibly de-identified) to the team to discuss as a group, or role play with an employee about a challenge they are having. Reinforce that politics are a reality, not an option, and that everyone can choose how to respond to these (sometimes unpleasant) realities.
14. **Introduce new responsibilities piece by piece**, such as having someone observe the process, then become a part of the team that completes it, and finally leading the team to complete the process. Provide opportunities for staff to ask questions and provide feedback.
15. **Provide staff with feedback frequently.** Your best staff will be hungry for feedback because they want to keep improving. Be specific; instead of saying, "This report looks great," instead say, "I like how you

made your three main points clearly and succinctly." Provide suggestions for improvement, such as, "If you were to do this again, I suggest you could xxx," or "This is great, and to make it even more effective, you could yyy." Continually provide honest praise--look for good things your staff are doing and let them know how much you appreciate them.

16. **Ensure staff are engaged and not bored.** Keeping them busy with projects to complete helps them stay focused on their work.
17. **Help your staff advocate for themselves.** If you see it's time for your staff to get a raise or promotion, help them identify how and advocate with them.

See also:
Chapter 1: Be the Boss You Always Wanted
Chapter 6: Communicating Like a Boss
Chapter 9: Conducting Performance Reviews

Chapter 4: Delegating

A big challenge many new bosses have is learning to delegate work to others and following up on it. Follow these suggestions, practice, and become a master delegator.

1. **Start small.** It's hard to let go of big tasks when you're responsible for their completion. Delegate small items first. Check back in to ensure they are being completed appropriately. And give clear, precise feedback until the work is done to your standards.
2. **Clarify your expectations.** This is often a communication challenge, especially if you are not sure what you want. For more junior/less experienced staff, be very concrete, including seemingly simplistic details (for example, the font, the margins, etc.). You may even want to outline what you're looking for in writing so they can complete the outline. For more experienced staff, you can give more general expectations, such as "I want a 2-page report that will explain our activities over the past year," and they can figure out the steps to get what you're looking for.
3. **Give a timeline.** Let your staff know when you expect them to have completed part or all of the

project and let them know how to get it to you. For example, you could say, "I'd like to see an outline of the report on Friday, with the final report a week from Friday. Please email me the draft and free up a half hour on Friday for us to review the outline."

4. **Follow up to ensure tasks are completed correctly.** You might want to schedule a halfway point check-in so you can see progress. If progress hasn't been made or is not what you're looking for, clarify your expectations.

5. **Praise what your staff did well and provide corrections and direction in a positive way.** Most people are trying to do what you're asking them to do, and it's often best to be positive when you know someone is trying. If you feel like someone isn't giving you their best work or is blowing you off, ask them about it instead of responding harshly. You could say, "I've seen your completed work with much more detail and accuracy than this. Was there something going on this week that you couldn't give this your usual high level of attention?" Give them a chance to explain.

6. **If tasks are not done how you want them, clarify what you're looking for and ask the person to give it another try.** You may want to suggest your staff ask someone else to review their work and provide feedback so they can revise before they send it to you.

That also helps teach two people about asking for and receiving feedback!

7. **Clarify your priorities.** Staff who are completing multiple tasks may understandably get confused when they're asked to do many things at once. Let them know what deadlines you have and how to prioritize tasks. Let them know they can check in with you if they have any questions.

8. **Teach new skills.** You can't expect your staff to know everything you do, and you might need to teach them or at least help them learn. If it becomes clear someone doesn't know how to do something, either show them or direct them to a resource or peer so they can learn. Many companies offer training in skills such as managing spreadsheets and basic programming; there are also videos online that individuals can watch and then ask you questions about. Build time into your request if the person needs training or coaching on a new skill.

9. **Play to your staff's strengths and give learning opportunities depending on the urgency of the project.** Ideally, there is plenty of time for everything to be a learning opportunity with lots of attention from you to ensure they get it right. In reality, however, we often don't have time to do as much training and mentoring as we'd like. When there's an urgent task, give it to the person who can get it done

quickly and correctly. Save learning opportunities for times when you have more flexibility.
10. **Ask staff for feedback.** The goal is to have a smooth process where you delegate tasks with clear expectations and timelines, and the staff can address your requests accurately and timely. If you're not providing enough information to them, or they feel confused by what you're asking for, work to clarify and provide more support. If their feedback is negative, this will give you options for how to improve.

See also:
Chapter 6: Communicating Like a Boss
Chapter 7: Acing Difficult Conversations
Chapter 8: Asserting Your Authority

Chapter 5: Supervising Someone Older Than You

I have had the exciting and intimidating experience of supervising people older than me. It is definitely challenging to be in charge of a team at 25 years old when everyone else on the team is in their 30s and 40s. As a Millennial boss, you are likely to run into this issue. Often. Read on . . .

1. **Communicate effectively, which includes both speaking <u>and</u> listening.** Many times, we speak too much because we want others to understand how capable we are. Unfortunately, this can result in staff of any age feeling their ideas and perspectives are being dismissed, especially older staff who bring years of experience.
2. **Leverage the strengths of your team.** Your older staff have more experience than you, as well as unique talents and strengths. Find a way to identify what they uniquely bring to the table, recognize their gifts, and incorporate their strengths into the conversation.
3. **Eliminate age-related statements and self-deprecating humor among your team.** Become aware of how others will react to statements like, "I'm old enough to be your mother," or "I wasn't

born when 9/11 happened." Although these statements may be accurate, even when staff are joking, it can rub people the wrong way unnecessarily. It also sends the message that age is an okay thing to discuss at work, when it's generally not.

4. **Put your team and the mission first.** Although it might feel important to have the right title, the larger office, or to speak up first in the meeting, it may be more impactful to identify what's best for the team and the mission. Your strength will be noticed.

5. **Consider how to address questions or comments about your age or appearance.** Although people aren't supposed to ask these questions, someone will inevitably ask you how old you are or if you remember cultural events that happened before you were born. Consider how you feel about the questions, and make sure you have a prepared answer or at least a playful deflection. If you think such questions might throw you off guard, practice with a friend or in front of a mirror so you can answer nonchalantly or at least without frustration or anger. I once had an employee reply angrily to a request, "I'm old enough to be your mother!" Thankfully, my response was ready: "It's really not appropriate for *either* of us to talk about age in the workplace."

6. **Aim for respect, not for being liked.** This is a developmental task for most of us in our 30s, but as

a boss supervising older staff, it's critical. Regardless of your age, if you let your staff walk all over you, they will no longer respect you. Do the right thing, stay tough, and hold your ground.

7. **Consider how you present to others.** One day when I was rushing around trying to put out another fire, my boss stopped me in the hallway and said, "When you act anxious, your staff will feel anxious. When you act calm, they will feel calm." #truth. This has been a valuable lesson to me as a boss.

8. **Consider whether it would be worthwhile to modify your hair, piercings, tattoo visibility, or wardrobe.** I'm not suggesting you totally change your entire appearance, but sometimes minor adjustments can be effective in facilitating how you want to be viewed while still feeling authentic to you.

9. **Teach your staff *and* learn from them.** We all have something to learn. For everything you bring to the table in energy, innovation, or whatever your unique superpowers, your staff have experience, political savvy, knowledge of others, and so much more to teach you.

10. **When you feel self-doubt, recall other times where you started something ambitious and completed it--whether high school sports, an art project, college, basic military training, or something else.** Stay focused, open to learning, authentic, and diplomatic, and things will be okay.

11. **Remember your value.** Don't let anyone (anywhere) diminish your sense of self-worth for any reason, especially not because of your age. You are in this role because you have a lot to offer and because someone believes in you enough to hire you. Do your thing, seek consultation when needed, and know that you're in control.

See also:
Chapter 4: Delegating
Chapter 6: Communicating Like a Boss
Chapter 8: Asserting Your Authority

Chapter 6: Communicating Like a Boss

Many of us speak and communicate without giving it a second thought. Although that tends to work out pretty well with people we know, who know us, and who have similar values, it's useful for communication with diverse populations to be more intentional.

1. **Interpersonal communication involves the exchange of information, ideas, and feelings between people through verbal or nonverbal means.** Of course, what we intend and what is received are not always completely in alignment. With people who are different from us (e.g., race, country of origin, gender), we may have to work harder to be fully understood. For example, think of the last time you were misunderstood by someone. How did you feel? What could you have done differently to be a bridge builder for understanding in that situation?
2. **Communication can lead to conflict when we arrive with our perceptions while failing to acknowledge that our perceptions are always never entirely accurate.** Remember, we form our own reality based upon what we see, and we can never fully see the entire picture. This leads to conflicts in communication where the message, unlike on the

commercial, is not heard.

3. **When communicating, it's important to remember that we show respect for others.** Showing respect means treating people who may be different the way you wish to be treated. Snide remarks or casting "shade" does not exemplify respect for others. Have you ever been disrespected simply for being who you are? How did you feel?

4. **Work on transparency as much as possible within the boundaries of appropriate cultural communication.** Americans typically communicate directly, verbally, assertively, and persuasively in their speech. When working with a more diverse group, however, it's important to respect other methods of communication. And of course, pay attention to the nonverbal communication – the person you're communicating with probably is!

5. **Learn to accept responsibility for your behavior.** All of us fumble every now and then. We may say the wrong thing or make the wrong assumptions when it comes to people who are different than we are. The important thing is that we pick the ball up once it's dropped. And then we must make sure that once we pick the ball up, we handle it properly. Remember, connecting and communicating are key!

6. **Remember for every action there is a reaction.** This is true when you connect with others in your workplace and beyond. When you connect with

others, expect there to be a response. While you can't ultimately control the response of the other person, you can certainly have a great impact by thinking through your communication and how you connect with others who are different.

7. **One huge misstep when it comes to connecting and communicating is our tendency to generalize.** It's important to approach each individual and each situation from an objective point of view. This is called cultural relativism. It's when we attempt to place ourselves in the shoes of the other person and see the world from their point of view rather than our own.

8. **Remember the way you connect and communicate with others allows you to send both verbal and nonverbal messages that shape the behavior of others**. Because your communication has the power to shape others, you have the power to effect change in the culture. You can send positive, empowering, and supportive messages that lift people up, or send negative, disempowering messages. You get to choose.

9. **Often we say that we want growth, but we do not have a growth mindset.** Before you can communicate change, you must think and believe that change is possible. There's no use in waking up in the morning and dreading going to work. It's important to adopt and maintain a positive mindset.

Think of ways you can be positive – and communicate positivity -- even when discouraging situations arise.
10. **Include everyone to the extent you can.** Sometimes we leave people out if we feel they may not be interested or if they have a reputation for being difficult. But if you're going to communicate effectively, it's important to include all team members and stakeholders when you can. Make a point to be inclusive, even when it's difficult. You'll be respected more for it.

See also:
Chapter 1: Be the Boss You Always Wanted
Chapter 7: Acing Difficult Conversations
Chapter 11: Motivating Staff

Chapter 7: Acing Difficult Conversations

This section provides some guidance on how to have these difficult conversations in a way that is respectful while staying curious to identify how to best proceed. Keep your values and goals in mind for difficult conversations. For more information, see the classic books *Difficult Conversations: How to Discuss What Matters Most* by Douglas Stone, Bruce Patton & Sheila Heen and *Crucial Conversations: Tools for Talking When Stakes Are High* by Al Switzler, Joseph Grenny, Kerry Patterson, and Ron McMillan.

1. **Don't avoid difficult conversations.** As author Tim Ferris said, "A person's success in life can usually be measured by the number of uncomfortable conversations he or she is willing to have."
2. **First identify what the issue is and what you would like the resolution of this conversation to be.** Maybe you're having a problem with a colleague, and you want to discuss it with a mentor. Find a way to describe the colleague problem succinctly, and ask for what you would like from the mentor. You could say, "I'd like to hear several ways to approach this situation" or "I'd like to hear what you would do if you were me."

3. **Recognize that in every conversation there is often a difference between what people think, what they say, and (if the conversation takes place in writing) what they write.** Starting with you, try to track the difference between what you say and what you're thinking. Keep in mind there are often comments you may think that should not be *said* or *written* at work.
4. **Consider that we all have different experiences because we focus on different things,** and we interpret the same events differently based on our past experiences and our values. For example, you and your boss may differ on what is meant by a "draft" report, and you may turn in something more "drafty" than your boss wanted.
5. **Approach each difficult conversation with a goal of each person getting some of what they wanted.** If you approach as all-or-nothing (you get everything you wanted and they get nothing), you are much less likely to have productive conversations (or to get what you want from them) in the future.
6. **Demonstrate that you are trying to understand what the other person is saying.** Pay attention, nod, or let them know how you are interpreting what they are saying. For example, you could say, "I want to make sure I understand. You are saying . . . ?" You could also elicit their perspective by asking something like,

"I know you wanted to discuss our relationship. Why do you think it's tense?"

7. **Blame is not generally helpful** if you're looking for an answer or for a change. Blame also makes it look like you're not trying to resolve the situation, only trying to avoid responsibility. Try to stay away from blame and stick to the point.
8. **Whenever possible, use data to support your points.** Look up the information about how these situations are typically handled and the expected outcomes of how you propose to handle the situation.
9. **Be careful of taking action based on assumptions.** It's often best to go into a difficult conversation with a lot of questions about the other person's behavior or intentions. If you want to share with the person the impact of their behavior on you, you could say, "When [x] happened, I assumed [y]. Is that true?" or "When you [x], it was confusing to me. Could you help me understand what you meant?"
10. **You may want to practice difficult conversations with a friendly partner** beforehand. Anticipate what the other person might say and practice how you might respond to various comments.
11. **Consider the extent to which you let your feelings be involved** in the conversation. Some people suggest all work conversations should be objective and emotionless; others (like me) believe that it's okay to let people know how you feel. ("I wanted to talk with

you about yesterday's meeting. When you called me out, I felt embarrassed. Can we discuss how to do this differently next time?") It is important to not let your feelings take over.

12. **If you get upset or angry in a conversation, you can ask for a break** or suggest you continue the conversation at another time. That's a better choice than crying or yelling at someone. If you do cry or raise your voice, ask for a break and then go back to the conversation when you're more composed.

13. **Observe difficult conversations**--in person, in movies, eavesdropping on the subway--and identify what works well and what doesn't.

14. **Recognize that you will make mistakes**--we all do. Pick yourself up, identify what you learned, and keep going.

See also:
Chapter 6: Communicating Like a Boss
Chapter 8: Asserting Your Authority
Chapter 13: Building Belonging

Chapter 8: Asserting Your Authority

Some people just exude authority, whereas others of us have to work at it. It's important when you're the boss to assert your authority so people feel confident following your leadership. Here are some ways that people of any age can assert their authority.

1. **Know and believe your origin story.** Clarify your story of who you are, either by drafting a personal statement or practicing it. It's important to have this story not just because you'll need a personal statement at some point, but because it changes how you think of yourself. Whether you're a scrappy go-getter, someone confident who always knows what they want, or something else, clarifying who you authentically are and sharing your story can help you stride through your workplace with authority.
2. **Clarify and share your mission.** As important as it is to know who you are, it's also important to know why you're here. Are you at this job to make a difference, to learn everything, to support and mentor others? Clarify your big, bold mission that you're passionate about and share it when appropriate.
3. **Pay attention to how you present yourself.** Many people stumble on their words when they're

uncomfortable and use lots of um's and pauses. This does not inspire confidence. Practice public speaking at Toastmasters or at work so you can present yourself – even when you're put on the spot – with authority.

4. **Watch your nonverbal communication.** Are you hopping from leg to leg when you stand up and talk? Are you curling up into a ball, or twirling your hair, or always looking down? If your nonverbal and verbal communication are at odds, you're not going to be effective.

5. **Watch your tone.** Aim to present with a calm and strong tone of voice. Do not yell or lose your cool, especially if you're young, a woman, or a person of color (or any combination of these). When some people yell they are perceived as passionate; for the rest of us, we are interpreted as being out of control and unprofessional.

6. **Do your homework.** It's much easier to assert your authority when you know what you're talking about. Study, read, interview experts … if you want to be awesome, it takes some work!

7. **Keep conflict impersonal.** Conflict should always be focused on resolving the situation, not on the people, personalities, or emotions involved. Keep the goal of solving the problem and ensuring fairness. Learn de-escalation skills if you're hot-headed or if some of your staff are.

8. **Praise in public, correct in private.** Don't correct people in public unless there's an emergency. Shaming people or embarrassing them is not a good strategy for building skills and teamwork. Do praise the heck out of them – tell them frequently that you appreciate their hard work, attentiveness, dedication, and skill. Watch their faces light up when they see you genuinely appreciate them!
9. **Develop strong networks and relationships.** When colleagues have your back and you have theirs, it's easier to walk the halls with pride. When you have colleagues you can learn from and grow with, you will maintain loyalty to each other beyond this job and position. You never know when you'll meet someone again; building and maintaining positive relationships with like-minded people will serve you well.
10. **Keep your integrity.** Take a stand when you need to, be diplomatic when you must, and be authentic. Always.

See also:
Chapter 1: Be the Boss You Always Wanted
Chapter 7: Acing Difficult Conversations
Chapter 14: Using Your Power for Good

Chapter 9: Conducting Performance Reviews

In the U.S., there is strong belief in meritocracy, which is the idea individuals with more skills, education, talent, and hard work reap greater benefits than those without. Unfortunately meritocracy is a myth, and many wonderful people with skills, education, talent, and hard work are passed over, unseen, or unrecognized. You have an opportunity as a boss to provide feedback, to help your staff improve, to help them reach their goals and to mentor them, all through the humble performance review process.

1. **Understand that companies, the U.S., and the world are not meritocracies.** Although they may claim to promote people and ideas based on merit, there are still too many underlying factors for this to be realized fairly. Also understand that believing the context is a meritocracy leads people to *think* they are fair, when they are actually more likely to be unfair. For example, women and race/ethnic minority men in the same jobs, with the same performance review, receive lower salary increases than white men. That is not meritocracy. Providing formal, accurate, and honest performance reviews is one small way to try to make the world a little fairer.

2. **Performance reviews are stressful endeavors for both supervisors and staff.** Ensure all staff know what the expectations are, what success looks like, and whether raises or bonuses are riding on the performance review. Evaluate people only on factors they can control; organizations should take responsibility for the factors that are out of the staff's control. Whether someone has competitive/supportive colleagues, a capable/not as capable boss, sufficient/insufficient opportunity for visibility and plum assignments should be taken into account in performance reviews. This will also help mute the myth of meritocracy by specifically calling out specific factors not in the person's control.
3. **Performance reviews should never be a surprise.** Ideally, managers and supervisors are providing feedback throughout the entire performance period. If you're waiting until an annual performance review to give critical feedback, you're too late. Ideally check in at least once a quarter. Have the difficult conversation, provide support or training, and help the employee be successful as soon as you see a problem, not once a year.
4. **Encourage all staff and managers to give and receive feedback.** If the goal is to increase individual and team performance, all staff should feel free to offer feedback and suggestions, and all staff should be able to manage receiving feedback. Provide training if

necessary so this process stays successful and positive. Reward individuals who provide helpful and respectful feedback – and those who accept feedback professionally and use it to improve their work.

5. **Encourage self-evaluation**. Some employees feel insulted if they are asked to provide a written self-evaluation, but this strategy is helpful for supervisors to learn where expectations or perspectives of performance may differ. Explaining the self-evaluation as a critical professional development skill can make this into a better learning opportunity.

6. **… and 360-degree evaluations.** If your company supports them, consider 360-degree evaluation. In these evaluations, an assessor talks to or surveys your bosses, peers, and subordinates to provide a broader picture of how you are perceived.

7. **Strive for fairness and equity in performance reviews.** Incorporate best practices for fair performance reviews, including ensuring expectations are clear, working collaboratively with the staff to get an accurate perception of performance and challenges beyond their control, addressing each criterion, providing positive feedback as well as areas to improve, and giving overall direction to the staff.

8. **Also, if you're not getting a performance review…** talk to your boss. You can provide them with a

summary of your accomplishments and a self-assessment, you can find the review form and fill it out and ask for their feedback, or you can just ask informally for feedback. You have options!

See also:
Chapter 3: Developing and Retaining Strong Staff
Chapter 7: Acing Difficult Conversations
Chapter 10: Being an Ally, Advocate, and Mentor

Chapter 10: Being an Ally, Advocate, and Mentor

Many Millennials may think they're too young or too inexperienced to mentor someone else. That's a myth! Everyone has something to offer, including people junior to you, people at your level of seniority, and people senior to you. Similarly, regardless of your position or age, you can be an ally and an advocate. Yes, you can make the world better by helping others!

1. **The first step to becoming an ally, advocate, or mentor is to do your homework.** *Allies* speak up for people even when it's uncomfortable. *Advocates* publicly recommend and support others, especially when they're not there. *Mentors* provide career advice, training, and suggestions to another person. Allies, advocates, and mentors should make time to read, listen, watch, and deepen their understanding of others so that they can best be of service to others.
2. **If doing your homework seems exhausting, we understand.** To be fair, that is an experience many people have when they first start delving into the work of truly understanding others, especially related to diversity, equity, and inclusion. It's also fair to acknowledge that most people in the world don't have the choice to learn about sexism, racism,

homophobia, and so on because it is an everyday aspect of their life. *It's important to recognize that it is a privilege to be able to learn about diversity, equity, and inclusion at your own pace and from relative safety.*

3. **Lift as you climb.** In some organizations, knowledge is used as power and doled out only to certain people viewed as having earned it. Be generous with your knowledge and help people when you can.

4. **Be honest and clear in your availability and boundaries regarding your areas of expertise, time, availability, and style with mentees.** Give honest feedback to others, including if they are not holding up their side of mentoring, such as following up or scheduling meetings. And of course, deliver what you promise. When you first start a mentoring relationship, ask them to share what they are looking for and what they expect. Then you can both decide how you'd like to set up the relationship. For example, do you meet monthly in your office, or is the mentee free to text you any concerns or questions at any time?

5. **Recognize your own privilege.** To be an ally, mentor, and advocate, it's important to recognize your own advantages and privilege. It's also important to recognize that others have been denied these same advantages and privileges. This acknowledgement is difficult for many people because it suggests you didn't completely earn all of

your success. It can also be a source of shame for people, especially people who experienced less-visible adversity (such as childhood trauma) that they may still be processing. Shame makes it difficult to clearly see and accept privilege. In order to help others, it's important to recognize where they're coming from.

6. **... and use your privilege for good.** You can use your privilege as a white person or as a man (or many other identities that have privilege) to stand up for others who are not sure they will be heard and respected in the same way.

7. **Pay attention to how other groups experience meetings and other work events.** You may not realize the extent to which people are uncomfortable or not heard or minimized. For example, many of us experience having our contribution to a group be ignored but then when someone else makes the same point, it is praised. Consider how it might or might not be helpful to speak up. Ask the individual if you're not sure how best you can support them.

8. **When you see a problem, speak up.** Monitor your community and your workplace for racism, sexism, and homophobia, and speak up. Even if all you say is, "I'm not comfortable with this discussion," that's a step forward.

9. **Accept the responsibility of being an ally, advocate, and mentor.** It is an important responsibility to help

shape someone's career and to develop them as a person! You are responsible for holding others accountable to make sure that meetings happen, actions are completed, and targets are reached – that does not mean you do the work for them. Ensure you don't take on more responsibility than you can manage.

10. **Actively advocate for and promote others.** Mention to others how wonderful your colleagues and staff are, how hard they've been working, what they've achieved, or how proud of them you are. When your staff's name comes up, make sure to put in a good word.

11. **Allies, advocates, and mentors should be role models.** Assume your staff are observing you at work, because they are! Share the rewards and enthusiasm about work and be frank about your frustrations. Focus on both technical skills and "real life," such as what a week is typically like, how you balance work and life, or how you approach conferences. Communicate the importance of allyship, advocacy, and mentorship and your hope that your staff will pass it on.

12. **Let them make their own decisions.** Although you may think you know more about everything (!), telling them what to do will deprive them of the opportunity to learn. Focus on asking questions and provide feedback on their assumptions, thought

processes, and strategies rather than directing them what to do.

13. **If you need to end a mentoring relationship, be honest and clear about why and when and how.** I typically let my mentees know I'm available to them for the rest of our careers, but occasionally I need to end a mentoring relationship because the mentee isn't using our time well, is chronically unprepared, or I have exhausted what I have to give them. When this happens, I recommend sharing this information with them kindly, suggesting other mentors and possibly encouraging them to contact you if circumstances change.

14. **Enjoy being an ally, advocate, and mentor!** Delight in watching others learn and grow and increase their confidence. You are making a positive difference in the world by contributing to others' success and development.

See also:
Chapter 1: Be the Boss You Always Wanted
Chapter 3: Developing and Retaining Strong Staff
Chapter 13: Building Belonging

Chapter 11: Motivating Staff

"If you want to build a ship, don't drum up people to gather wood, divide the work, and give orders. Instead, teach them to yearn for the vast and endless sea." As Antoine de Saint-Exupery, author of *The Little Prince,* noted, motivating people can be an indirect and challenging endeavor. Nevertheless, staff will perform much better and be more satisfied when they are motivated.

1. **Humor can help put things in perspective, bring people together, relieve stress, increase engagement, improve morale, and increase creativity**. Using positive humor -- no put-downs of anyone -- can be as simple as starting a meeting by saying, "Does anyone have a good, clean joke?"
2. **Expressing appreciation for the work of your staff can work wonders**. Letting people know you see that they are working hard, pushing themselves, helping others, or otherwise doing a great job can motivate staff to persevere through difficult times. Be as specific as possible in describing exactly what they did and why it was so wonderful. You can also mix it up by letting people know individually verbally, writing a note, and sharing appreciation in a larger group. Praise the effort, the result, the creativity, the

persistence, or whatever they are doing well. Note progress when you see it and keep encouraging them to get even better.

3. **Help staff set and strive toward goals.** Help them identify what they want to learn (or if they're not clear on what they want to learn, what you think they *need* to learn to be successful). Find something they can get motivated about and help them take steps forward.

4. **Set an example.** Sometimes it's helpful to talk through steps out loud as you're doing them so the other person can understand your thought process. Saying, "Wow. This is so frustrating. I wonder what I could do differently to make this work better," is empowering to junior people because they see how to keep going despite feeling frustrated, and how to think through problems without losing motivation.

5. **Help staff see there's a connection between targeted hard work and success.** Check to see if they are working effectively -- not working hard only for the sake of working hard -- so their efforts are targeted toward the goals they want to achieve.

6. **Notice discouragement and pay attention to negative talk.** If you have staff who say, "I'm not really good at this," or "I don't know where to start," or "I don't know what to do," start asking questions. In a supportive way, you can find out what they need and help think through the task at hand. Ensure staff

understand they can let you know if they're struggling without being punished or feeling like this will be a strike against them. And notice when they're struggling and offer to help. I tell staff: "Don't suffer in silence. If you get stuck, ask me or someone else for help so we can help you work through it."

7. **Help staff understand the steps in sequence of operations** and implications of their particular role in the process. It's hard for junior people to see the big picture in complicated processes, including the steps in the process, who handles the step before their work, and who handles the step after their work. Helping them understand the big picture can improve their skills, help build their network, and also reduce isolation since they will see how critical their role is to the functioning of the whole team.

8. **Ensure staff have the proper training and the right tools for the job.** Help them understand what skills and tools are needed, and help them get the right ones.

9. **Protect them from bullying and harassment from others.** Be fiercely protective of your staff. If someone is harassing or bullying your staff -- even your staff they made a mistake -- talk with your staff and the bully about what is going on and help resolve the situation. Be clear that you do not tolerate disrespect.

10. **Help staff learn and grow.** When frustrating things happen, reassure staff that everyone makes mistakes and that our obligation is to learn from them. Ask them to tell you the steps they took to solve a problem, what their assumptions were, and how they made decisions. You can then ask them questions that challenge their observations, assumptions, or decisions. Ask questions to help them identify where things went wrong and how to do things better next time.

See also:
Chapter 3: Developing and Retaining Strong Staff
Chapter 6: Communicating Like a Boss
Chapter 8: Asserting Your Authority

Chapter 12: Building the Multicultural Workplace

Workplaces can be like families, where there is support for each other. They can also be like families in that there are lots of differences and people don't always get along. Work, however, is a place where it's important to get along. You don't have to like everyone, but you do have to be respectful and diplomatic and work together. If you see yourself on the management track, this is especially important.

Diverse cultures are creative cultures. These diverse cultures poised to produce new and innovative ideas. However, just because diverse cultures are creative and poised to produce new ideas doesn't mean that those ideas are actually implemented. Studies show that despite the ability to be innovative, diverse cultures are not always inclusive cultures. When individuals feel excluded, they withhold ideas. It is important that individuals on your team are encouraged and are comfortable sharing.

1. **Do what you can to create a culture of diversity and inclusion** by being respectful to everyone and not engaging in or tolerating disrespectful behavior.

2. **Check with your organization's diversity office or diversity-focused groups in your profession.** Identify how you and your team could get involved and learn.
3. **Check in with team members individually and regularly** about how any diversity issues in the office may be affecting them and find out how you can help.
4. **Be an ally, advocate and mentor to others more junior than you,** especially groups that are underrepresented in senior leadership. You always have something to offer, even if only support.
5. **Use pronouns and names that individuals request.**
6. **Understand that some people may not intend to be disrespectful and may just lack awareness or be culturally insensitive.** This doesn't mean that their behavior is acceptable; only that it's important not to assume negative intent. If someone is disrespectful to you or others, make it a priority to talk with them about it, and escalate if needed.
7. **Be aware that there are often stark differences by seniority and tenure at organizations.** Try to assume positive intent. For example, if you keep receiving menial assignments, instead of assuming it's because you're the youngest person, talk to your boss about your ability to do more challenging work. Someone has to do the menial work, though, and if you're the most junior, it might be you until someone more junior is hired or until you move up.

8. **Consider who's being promoted in your organization, and how promotion decisions are made.** Are promotions given to those who request them? Those who speak up? Those who spend long hours in the office? If so, you might be holding back some people, including those with softer communication styles, family needs for flexible hours, or people who are shyer about speaking up.
9. **Ensure that diverse members of your team are not assigned to menial tasks.** Diverse team members may feel overlooked or dismissed when given responsibilities that are unrewarding and mundane.
10. **Encourage your diverse staff and colleagues to take on challenges that reflect their skillset or that will enable them to learn new skills.** Show that you have already bought into their ability to contribute to the team and organization.
11. **Keep clear boundaries about violations, and also choose your battles.** Sometimes people say stupid or hurtful things, including ageist comments about Millennials and other younger or older team members. This is counterproductive.
12. **Share stories in your organization and with the community about successful individuals** who are women, members of minority groups, part of the LGBTQ community, or who are disabled. Invite individuals and groups to share their own experiences.

13. **Although it's important to speak your mind, sometimes it's more appropriate to observe the situation and ask questions or speak up later.** For example, if there is a very senior meeting with your boss, your boss's boss, and that person's boss too, that might not be the best time to ask a question or provide an insight unless specifically requested. There are political issues at play that you might not see. Instead, observe carefully and ask your boss questions privately later.
14. **Be open to feedback** on your own behavior if you are unintentionally disrespectful to someone.
15. **Speak with a mentor or trusted colleague** if you have concerns about the organization's approach to diversity.

See also:
Chapter 3: Developing and Retaining Strong Staff
Chapter 6: Communicating Like a Boss
Chapter 14: Using your Power for Good

Chapter 13: Building Belonging

People are naturally social creatures. Even those of us who are introverts acknowledge that a sense of belonging is essential. Whether it is a feeling of belonging in your immediate family, your neighborhood, a social organization or on your job, we need a sense of kinship with others if we are going to effectively engage and meet our goals — both personal and professional. Studies show that people tend to gravitate and feel a sense of belonging with those who they most identify. But in the workplace, it's important to remember that everyone 'belongs'. This is what it means to be inclusive and not just diverse. But how can you help create a sense of belonging, especially if you're not in management.

1. **Advocate for others who are different or who may feel marginalized because of their identity.** It's easy to be silent, but it's much more challenging and advantageous to suggest that the hijab that your neighbor or co-worker wears is not a disturbance or distraction as some may claim. You can speak up and let others know how important it is that she is comfortable in her attire so that she can feel like she belongs. As a result, she will perform better. Advocate for others, and everybody wins.
2. **Suggest that the company start affinity groups (also known as employee resource groups.)** Affinity

groups bring people from within the company with shared interests. It's a great way for employees to know that the company cares about them holistically and not just what they do while sitting at their desk during the day.

3. **Present management with a few statistics.** Management loves to know how the bottom line of the company will be affected by new initiatives. Studies show that employees with a high sense of belonging take 75% fewer sick days than those who feel as if they're excluded. Employees also have a 50% higher turnover rate when they feel excluded, and they are 25% less productive in working toward the goals of their team. Those are important numbers for management to pay attention to!

4. **Be intentional about cultivating relationships with people who are not like you.** You can make a list of individuals you come in contact with and be deliberate about speaking to them or even asking them out to lunch. Regularly journal how your interactions turned out. Were they positive or negative? Why do you think they turned out the way they did? What did you learn about the other person? What did you learn about yourself?

5. **When people feel isolated, they lose a sense of purpose.** It's important that you, along with your co-workers, eradicate isolation and replace it with intentional actions designed to let others know that

they are valued and that they belong to the team.
6. **Consider online organization or public communities**. These communities can include your company's internal Slack, Jabber, or Google instant messaging services, or public Twitter, LinkedIn, Instagram, or other social media to connect with others. Reach out and build relationships!
7. **Consider a formal or informal mentorship.** Often new people who are struggling to belong are looking for a one-on-one relationship where they can gradually get to know the company and others. You can always be an ally or advocate even without a formal arrangement.
8. **Periodically reassess your role in your organization toward building belonging.** How are you helping others fit in, contribute to the team, and reach their potential? What else can you do to help?

See also:
Chapter 7: Acing Difficult Conversations
Chapter 10: Being an Ally, Advocate, and Mentor
Chapter 12: Building the Multicultural Workplace

Chapter 14: Using Your Power for Good

Whatever privilege and power you may have – as a supervisor or through your personal characteristics – use it for good.

1. **Know yourself, learn your power.** Identify strengths in your story and in the story of your culture and your people, such as persistence, collegiality, grit, or kindness. What strengths do your people, your culture, and you bring to the table? Regardless of the adversity or privilege you and your ancestors experience, you have power. Recognize your power and use it to help others.
2. **Recognize how you – or people who look or act like you – have hurt others or been hurt.** This will help you understand how you can be seen by others. All of us have at some time been unfair or unkind. Many of us have ancestors or parents who have intentionally or unintentionally benefited from and supported an unfair system. You don't have to feel guilty for everything any ancestor did; however, recognizing your people's role in others' oppression can inspire us to learn better and do better.
3. **Learn about others.** The more you learn about other cultures and ways of being, the more you can

recognize the strengths in everyone and in all aspects of their identity. Understanding these strengths – and a lifelong insistence on looking for them in everyone you meet – will improve your ability to relate to others.

4. **Accept that the system that facilitates privilege and oppression also works against those who try to make changes.** Although people who are privileged are also affected by the oppressive systems, in the form of fear, defensiveness, and lack of connection, it is often in the interests of the privileged to continue the current system. The dominant groups don't generally view these problems as *their* problems. Further, addressing these issues is challenging because there is fear about what will happen when the systems begin to change. You can work to change minds of individual people – and at the same time work to change the systems that facilitate privilege and oppression.

5. **There is increasing language and space for all people to have these conversations.** As we've stated many times, do your own homework. Learn the language of diversity, equity and inclusion so you can start to name things as they are. This will help you …

6. … **Become a truth-teller.** The more solidly you know who you are, what your culture is, and who your people are, and the more intimately you understand others and the culture and the language,

the more you can become a truth-teller who will communicate your observations and recommendations. Truth-tellers operate in the realm of candor, and model exceptionally high standards for equity and fairness. Further, and most important, truth-tellers encourage us to be better.

7. **Recognize the power in others and help them find their own power.** You don't need to become a savior of others to help them find their own power. Once you identify power in others, help them discover what is amazing and powerful about them. Help them see the strength in their culture and their ancestors and the potential for greatness in all of us. This will never be wasted energy.

See also:
Chapter 1: Be the Boss You Always Wanted
Chapter 10: Being an Ally, Advocate, and Mentor
Chapter 12: Building the Multicultural Workplace
Chapter 13: Building Belonging

ACKNOWLEDGEMENTS

We would like to thank reviewers Amanda Brooks, Kelly Farrow, Lindsay Harris, Reginald Madden, Tanida Mullen, Gerry Vogel, and Valerie Weaver. We appreciate Diego G. Diaz for cover design and photography, Wendy C. Garfinkle for publishing support, and Cassandra Blake for exemplary administrative assistance.

ABOUT THE AUTHOR

Jennifer Wisdom, PhD MPH ABPP, is a former academician who is now an author, consultant, speaker, and principal of Wisdom Consulting. As a consultant, she helps curious, motivated, and mission-driven professionals to achieve their highest potential by identifying goals and then providing them with the roadmap and guidance to get there. Jennifer is the author of the *Millennials' Guides* series, including *Millennials' Guide to Work*, *Millennials' Guide to Management & Leadership*, *Millennials and Generation Z Guide to Voting*, *Millennials' Guide to Relationships*, and *Millennials' Guide to the Construction Trades*.

Jennifer is a licensed clinical psychologist and board-certified business/organizational psychologist. She has worked with complex health care, government, and educational environments for 25 years, including serving in the U.S. military, working with non-profit service delivery programs, and as faculty in higher education. She is an intrepid adventurer based in New York City and Portland, Oregon. She can be reached at www.leadwithwisdom.com.

www.ingramcontent.com/pod-product-compliance
Lightning Source LLC
Chambersburg PA
CBHW071510070526
44578CB00001B/496